THIS BOOK is to
commemorate the issuance of the
official Oneida medal
March 15, 1974
and is limited to 15,000 copies
No. *7887*

Purcell Powless

Photograph by Henry F. Dobyns

THE EPISCOPAL CHURCH of the Holy Apostles, Oneida, Wisconsin. Completed in 1897, this church was severely damaged by lightning in 1921, rebuilt and rededicated in 1922.

THE

ONEIDA

PEOPLE

by Cara E. Richards

Scientific Editor: Henry F. Dobyns
General Editor: John I. Griffin

PUBLISHED BY INDIAN TRIBAL SERIES / PHOENIX

Copyright 1974
by
Indian Tribal Series

Library of Congress Catalog Number 74-82006

PRINTED IN THE UNITED STATES OF AMERICA — Imperial Lithographers

PURCELL R. POWLESS

E lected Tribal Chairman of the Oneida Tribe of Indians of Wisconsin in July of 1967, Purcell R. Powless won re-election in 1972 to a term extending to 1975. Besides serving as elected leader of the Wisconsin Oneida people, Mr. Powless acts as Senior Planner of the Oneida Tribe's Comprehensive Planning Program, a federally funded activity.

Purcell Richard Powless was born on Christmas Day in 1925 on the Oneida Indian Reservation. This son of Mark M. Powless, who himself served as chairman of the Oneida Tribe of Wisconsin, and Margaret Stevens Powless bears a name long well-known among the Iroquois peoples. He has four brothers and four sisters.

As a youth, Purcell Powless attended the Pipestone Indian School in Minnesota, and graduated from Flandreau Indian Vocational High School in South Dakota. As soon as he completed high school in 1943, young Powless joined the United States merchant marine for the duration of the second World War.

On December 28, 1945, Powless married Angeline Skenandore, a member of another very well-known Iroquois family. They have reared a family of five boys and three girls; their four eldest children are married.

Purcell R. Powless followed a long-time Iroquois pattern of seeking a career off his reservation in relatively dangerous work. Iroquois child-rearing customs produce adults with relatively little fear of heights, so many men work at building bridges and skyscrapers. Mr. Powless joined this group, living in the Milwaukee metropolitan area. There he has belonged to Local Number 8 of the International Bridge, Structural and Ornamental Ironworkers Union for twenty-six years. Not only Purcell, but also three of his brothers became steelworkers. His son Richard has followed in his footsteps working in high steel.

The Oneida tribal chairman found time to participate in other organizations, too. He serves on the Vestry of the Holy Apostles Episcopal Church in Oneida, and is a past Senior Warden there. He is also a Thirty-Second Degree Mason, and a member of the Master Mason Lodge in Seymour, Wisconsin, and the Tripoli Shrine Temple of Milwaukee. He also likes to hunt and fish, bowl and play golf.

As chairman of the Oneida Tribe, Mr. Powless serves on the Board of Directors of the Great Lakes Inter-Tribal Council. He is a member of the National Tribal Chairman's Association and the National Congress of American Indians.

Indian Tribal Series Photograph by Dan Zudell

MR. PURCELL R. POWLESS, Chairman of the Oneida Tribe of Indians of Wisconsin, Inc.

O *na yote ka o no.* The Granite People. People of the Rock. People of the Stone Set Up. *Onoichrhonons.* Oneidas. They might well be called the "Enduring People," as stone is enduring, for they still survive after the storms of centuries. Yet stone is too passive. The Oneidas have never been a passive people. Their history is full of courage, daring, and a readiness to change as well as the patience and endurance appropriate to a people called *O na yote ka o no.*

In one of the ironies of history, the Oneidas, who died with the colonists during the Revolution are less well known to modern Americans than their brother nations in the famous League of the Iroquois, the Mohawks and Senecas who fought for the British crown. Because the Oneidas were on the winning side, they did not figure in the heart-rending accounts of massacres nor in the exciting accounts of

1

captives. No American novels dwelt on their viciousness and ferocity. With casual disregard, white historians of European descent are too taken up with the saga of their colonial and pioneer ancestors to bother acknowledging their debt to the only true native Americans. Such historians pass over lightly Oneida heroism and courage.

Some Americans have heard the name "Oneida" associated with silver, ceramics or geographical locations. Yet most do not know that the Oneidas still exist as an embattled and proud people scattered across ancestral Iroquois homeland in New York State and defending new lands in Wisconsin against the always-eager white land-grabbers.

The story of how the Oneidas got to Wisconsin and what they are doing there is the theme of this book. It is a story full of the usual episodes of greed, treachery and betrayal that mar the history of relations between European and native American. At the same time, it is also a story of Oneida courage, self-sacrifice, vision and resourcefulness — qualities too often left unnoticed in the chronicles of American history.

This story opens, so far as history is concerned, in the winter of 1634-35, when a Dutch surgeon at Fort Orange (Albany) named Harmen Meyndersten van den Bogaert began a trip that led him into Oneida territory. He certainly was not the first European among the Oneidas, but he was the first to leave a detailed description of an identifiable Oneida town. Champlain attacked an Iroquois town in 1616, but

2

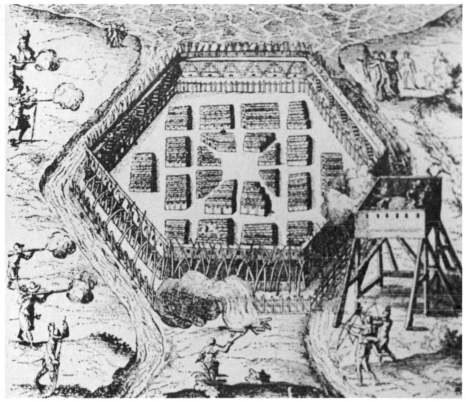

A FRENCH OFFICER'S SKETCH of an Iroquois palisaded settlement he saw in the early 17th century.

there is some question as to just where it was located and which nation inhabited it.

Dutchmen generally distinguished Mohawks, whom they called "Maquas," from other Iroquois, but lumped the other members of the League into a category called "Sinnekens." (Senecas). Van den Bogaert was the first Dutchman to make a distinction in print, mentioning Onondagas who came to council with the Dutchmen at the Oneida town called *Enneyuttehaga*. He also mentioned a song in which Onondagas, *Onneyatte* or Oneida and *Koyockure* or Cayuga were named.

Van den Bogaert arrived at the Oneida village December 30, 1634. The sixty-six lodges of *Enneyuttehaga* stood on a high hill, protected by a double palisade 767 paces in circumference with only two narrow entrances on the east and west. The wider western gate, three and a half feet, had three wooden man-like figures decorated with three scalps over it. The narrower two-foot wide entry was decorated with only one scalp and apparently no wooden figures.

Van den Bogaert had passed through Mohawk country on his way to Oneida. He did not repeat descriptions of things he had already mentioned, but simply described ways in which the Oneidas differed from Mohawks. Mohawk houses, he said, were flat-roofed bark structures up to one hundred feet long by twenty-two to twenty-three feet wide, aligned in rows separated by streets. Oneida houses were better, he said, wider and more finished. They

4

had wooden fronts painted with a variety of animals. He also said Oneidas slept on elevated boards, more than the other Indians he knew.

Just outside the town, Van den Bogaert noticed three graves which he described because they were the shape of European graves, not round as Iroquois graves usually were. They were enclosed in tight palisades painted in red, white and black. One that Van den Bogaert assumed to be the grave of a chief had its entrance topped with a large wooden bird and was decorated with paintings of various animals. According to later accounts, Oneidas were grouped into three large families or clans identified as Bear, Wolf and Tortoise or Turtle. Each of these included all individuals, even distant cousins, related through the female line. Family members assumed a special relationship with the animal their clan was named after. Individuals also often developed special relationships with spirits of other animals and birds. The decorations on Oneida houses and graves in 1634 likely represented special relationships or family memberships of house residents and grave occupants.

Mohawks and Oneidas were usually good hosts — a characteristic they maintain to this day. The Mohawks fed Van den Bogaert and his men venison, cornbread baked with beans, baked squash, bear meat, turkey and beaver. The Oneida diet differed slightly. Oneidas gave him more salmon and bear meat. He mentioned eating venison only once among the Oneidas, and turkey not at all.

In December, when the fall harvest was all

5

gathered but not yet appreciably depleted, Van den Bogaert saw houses full of maize and beans — more than 300 bushels of maize in some. There were Oneida houses with sixty or seventy or more dried salmon hanging in them. Van den Bogaert said six to eight fresh salmon were caught each day during his visit. Oneidas sold surplus fish to Mohawks. Van den Bogaert observed some female traders traveling through Mohawk country with green tobacco and dried fish for sale. They were asking one florin or two hands of *seawan* (wampum) for each fish. When they did not sell out in one settlement, they went on to the next.

Oneidas and Mohawks were eager to trade with the colonists as well as with each other. In one Mohawk town, Van den Bogaert met a man with 120 beaver skins for sale. He had hunted them with dogs, not trapped them as was later practice. A main topic of discussion with the Oneidas was trade. Van den Bogaert had no sooner arrived at *Enneyuttehaga* than a council member complained to him that Dutch prices for beaver were too low. He said French buyers gave six hands of *seawan* plus other presents. Van den Bogaert saw for himself the results of the visit of a French trade mission the previous August. Oneidas were wearing French shirts and coats and using French axes and razors.

Van den Bogaert himself was free with gifts on his trips. In return for the hospitality he received, he gave salt, tobacco, knives, needles, awls, scissors, axes and cloth, as well as ham and beer. The

6

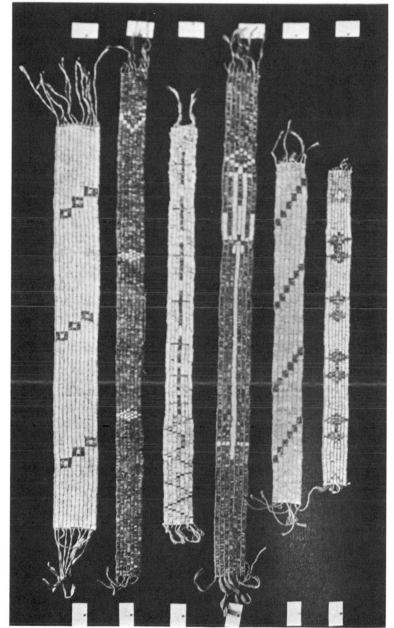

IROQUOIS CONDOLENCE BELTS, artistically fashioned from sea shells laboriously ground, drilled, and strung. Such strung shells became known as "wampum."

7

Mohawks and Oneidas for their part not only fed Van den Bogaert and his men whenever they stopped, but provided shelter and gave them food, furs, guides and interpreters for their trip. This hospitable treatment of friendly travelers was typical of Iroquois during the early days of contact but broke down later as the number of travelers increased and as colonial townsmen began demanding payment from native Americans, if they accepted them as guests at all.

When Van den Bogaert and his party arrived at Oneida Castle and *Enneyuttahaga* — they were lodged in a special house for holding councils and sheltering official guests. It was identified as the chief's house, but Van den Bogaert noted that it was not like an ordinary residence because no cooking was done there. Instead, large kettles of food were brought in from other houses three or four times a day. Council members ate there regularly, but anyone in the house when the food arrived also received some. If there were not enough bowls to go around, more were brought in from other houses. Empty bowls were refilled until the guest decided he had enough.

The main Oneida chief was away visiting the French to try to arrange a peace treaty when Van den Bogaert arrived, but returned the next day. The Oneidas wanted peace, he explained, so they could travel to areas where beaver were more plentiful.

On January 1, 1635, Van den Bogaert observed the chief giving his report to the council. After a long discussion, the Oneidas decided to make peace with the French for four years. This decision reveals a significant difference between Oneida and European concepts of treaties, of peace and war. Europeans assumed that a treaty assured permanent peace unless its conditions were broken. To them war was a temporary condition and peace the "normal" one. Oneidas apparently viewed peace as a temporary condition which continually had to be re-established or war would automatically resume. This view explains the constant Iroquois councils with New York officials to "renew the covenant chain." Europeans and their New World descendants never really understood this conceptual difference.

Van den Bogaert made ready to leave Oneida after this council, complaining that he and his party were being starved and generally mistreated. The Oneidas urged the Dutchmen to stay because they had invited Onondagas to come to council. They promised to take better care of their visitors and to prove it invited them to salmon and bear meat feasts twice that day.

Van den Bogaert may simply have been making a gesture, but it is possible that the party was being slighted. By no means all of the Iroquois were favorably inclined toward Dutch colonists. Only eight years before, in 1626, the latter had been at war with the Iroquois. The threat to the Dutch had been so severe that they evacuated Fort Orange civilians to New Amsterdam.

On Van den Bogaert's way to Oneida, an Iroquois

had tried to stab one member of his party. Van den Bogaert mentioned several times while at *Enneyut-tahaga* how easily the Oneidas could kill his group, although he did not expect it to happen. When he prolonged his visit, the Commissioner at Fort Orange sent him an alarmed note, and the Iroquois who brought it said people at the post were quite concerned, fearful that the whole party had been wiped out.

On January 3, before the Onondagas arrived, the Oneidas held a council with the Dutchmen. The first thing they did was to feel Van den Bogaert's heart beat to verify his statement that he was not afraid of them — a very early application of the lie-detector principle. When they were convinced he was not frightened, they got down to business. They officially complained, as a council member had remarked earlier, that the Dutch traders paid too little for beaver. The council proposed four hands of *seawan*, suggesting that the earlier demand for six might have been a profiteering attempt. It said that if the Dutch representatives would promise four hands of *seawan*, they would not trade anywhere else. They also asked that Dutch merchants stock a larger, more varied supply. They particularly wanted cloth, *seawan*, axes and kettles. Van den Bogaert did not promise anything except that he would take their complaints back to Fort Orange and return in the spring with an answer, but the Oneidas seemed satisfied. They gave him beaver skins and said he was now free to travel in *Onneyatte*, Onondaga, *Koyockure*

10

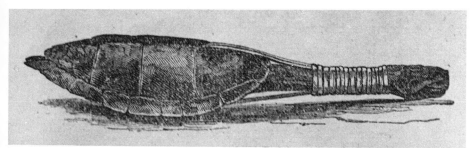

TURTLE NOT ONLY PROVIDED shell rattles for curing ceremonies and dances, but also was the totem of one Oneida clan.

AN EARLY ARTIST'S CONCEPTION of the appearance of an Iroquois "Long House" or communal dwelling for several families.

and *Tiolohalton*, which may have been Seneca country. They even offered to guide him to New France if he cared to go.

The next day, two Oneidas invited Van den Bogaert to a curing ceremony "to drive away the devil"— revealing that Oneidas, like other native Americans, blamed sickness on supernatural intervention. Most of the active participants were men wearing red paint on their faces, which Van den Bogaert said was customary on important occasions. Three of the men wore wreathes braided of deer hair and an herb root. Five white crosses decorated the wreathes. This form of headdress was never described again, although the Jesuits who came a generation later would have been sure to notice the crosses. There is no archeological evidence of use of the cross before contact. In view of later Oneida conversion, this early appearance of the central symbol of Christianity among them constitutes a significant portent.

During the 1635 ceremony, an old woman kept up a rhythmic beat with a turtle-shell rattle while the men sang and danced. One of the dancers approached the sick man, sucked something from his neck and back and spat it into the mouth of an otter, that he then threw on the floor. A stuffed otter skin is used much this same way in the modern Ojibwa *medewiwin*. Sucking out the cause of illness has a worldwide distribution as a form of treatment. Other men began to throw fire, handle hot coals and ashes and even put fire in their mouths. The flying sparks

12

made Van den Bogaert so uneasy that he abruptly left.

The Onondagas, six old men and four women, finally arrived and the council was held January 11. It was much like the earlier Oneida council. The Onondagas gave Van den Bogaert fourteen beaver skins, asked him to visit Onondaga and complained about the Dutch price for beaver.

The council and individual conversations show clearly that the Iroquois already appreciated the rivalry between the European colonial powers. They were prepared to use it for their own advantage, foreshadowing their later diplomatic success with the technique. Not only did the Onondagas suggest that the Dutchmen had better pay more than the French traders if they wanted to attract Iroquois trade, but they rubbed the message in. They offered to take Van den Bogaert around Onondaga territory if he returned in summer to show him where Frenchmen brought trade goods by goat, thus saving the Onondagas a long trip. Van den Bogaert was noncommital and concluded the council by giving knives, awls and needles to the Onondaga.

Van den Bogaert and his party left for home the next day. At their departure, an incident occurred that sheds light on another basic difference between Iroquois and European attitudes. The Dutch party had added twenty beaver skins, five salmon and some bread to their supplies. They wanted the Oneidas to carry their goods. With plenty of personal supplies to carry, the Oneidas did not see why the Dutchmen should not carry their own, a perfectly reasonable point of view for equalitarian people but strange to the class-structured Europeans. It took lengthy negotiations to settle the argument.

As they left for Fort Orange, the Oneidas asked the Dutchmen to fire their guns, and the latter obliged. This was a request made so often that Van den Bogaert had to limit compliance to special occasions. Iroquois seemed to take a particular pleasure from hearing gunfire not directed at them.

The Van den Bogaert journal provides one of the most complete descriptions of early contact between Oneidas and Europeans. The Oneida way of life had already begun to change. Smallpox had started its deadly work. At the first Mohawk village, the party had been forced to shelter in a small cabin a quarter of a mile away from the village because so many people there had died. The three Oneida graves may have resulted from the same epidemic. European trade items had reached the village in some quantity. Van den Bogaert described iron chains, hoops, nails and harrow irons in Mohawk country in addition to the French trade goods he saw at Oneida and things he brought himself. In their complaints, the Oneidas showed their desire for specific European goods. Negotiations with Dutch, French and more distant Indians all indicated an Oneida awareness of the mechanisms of trade and a readiness to engage in it.

According to archeological discoveries, this interest or ability to engage in travel and distant trade was a comparatively recent development. Iroquois

14

had been rather isolated prior to contact with Europeans. Archeological evidence and Iroquois tradition both suggest that, surrounded by hostile peoples, Iroquois were not able to engage in extensive trading expeditions until Europeans introduced new factors into the situation in native America.

The year 1635 seems to have been a significant one for the Oneidas. In the Jesuit Relation for that year, Father Jean Brebeuf named the *Onoiochrhonons* (Oneidas) as one of the five nations the Frenchmen included under the name *Hiroquois*. That is, by 1635 the French colonials recognized that there were five separate people who for some purposes could be considered as one. Frenchmen continued to use the single term *Hiroquois* as well as individual national names. The fact that both Dutch and French colonials consistently lumped at least four of the five nations under a single term supports those who believe that the League of the Five Nations already existed.

Europeans and their American descendents have failed to comprehend that the nature of power and authority in native American societies in general and Iroquois nations in particular never followed a European pattern. The League was a confederation and not an empire. As long as individual members of each Nation and all the Nations together agreed on what should be done, the League acted with power and decision. When there were differences of opinion that could not be overcome, leading to disagreements about the proper course of action, individual

15

Nations and even individuals within Nations could and did go their separate ways. The founding of the League, whenever it occurred, set up a mechanism for reaching group decisions and for settling conflicts between member Nations or between members and peoples outside the League. It did not set up any mechanism for enforcing the decisions reached, and depended entirely on voluntary compliance.

During the historic period, League members often disagreed, sometimes to the point of violence with each other, and they frequently acted independently. This individual action and even conflict never made a permanent breach, however, and the Nation that went its own way was either soon followed by the others or gave up its unilateral action. The League endures to this day in spite of all the conflicts, disagreements, separate actions, disruptions and the loss of territorial integrity.

The appearance of Europeans certainly introduced new elements into the situation. Differences in opinion about the Europeans and how to deal with the problems, novelties and new opportunities they presented increased the occasions for dissention within and between the different Iroquois Nations. Some of this is clearly apparent from the difficulty European Nations had in making and especially in maintaining peace.

Throughout the next two centuries until after the American Revolution, the history of Iroquois-colonial relations is littered with peace treaties, peace councils, and protests about violations of agreements. The situation was incredibly complex. Some European colonial was sponsoring a council somewhere in Iroquois territory every year, inviting individual Iroquois Nations to go to war against rival European powers, to come to a peace council, to give up prisoners, to accept missionaries, to reject missionaries, to accept traders, to reject traders, to cede land, to refuse to cede land, to accept the sovereignty of one king or to reject another. Individual Iroquois were swayed one way or another and individual Nations followed suit as one or another influential individual succeeded in persuading a council to decide in favor of his position, only to have the whole process begin again as some other influential individual began a campaign to reverse the decision, or a young man on his way to becoming influential led a war party out in defiance of a council decision.

Only one policy remained constant during all those years of turmoil. The Iroquois Nations never attacked New York colonists, either Dutch or English, after the brief war in 1626 until the American Revolution. Englishmen in other colonies might be attacked, killed, or made prisoner, but the New York colonists were safe. Defectors from this policy had no option but exile and had to move to French villages where they usually lost their original national identity.

One of the first French settlements that served as a haven for defectors was a mission station established in 1669 by Father Pierre Raffeix, a Jesuit, at La Prairie de la Magdelene on the south bank of the St.

Lawrence River opposite Montreal. He called it St. Francis Xavier de Pres and within a year sixty people had settled there, most of them Oneidas. It was a threat to New York colonists for decades.

A prime mover in helping to set up this mission station was Catherine Gandiaktena, an Erie captive who had been given to the Oneidas. Her life was spared and she married, but whether she married an Oneida or another captive is not clear. Her influence is only one early example of the effect displaced people were beginning to have even on those societies that held their territory and maintained their independence longest.

The story of displaced people, how they were absorbed and became true Oneidas is one of the most interesting aspects of the Oneida saga. Without these immigrants, Oneidas would have disappeared as a people. Yet, overwhelmed in numbers by outsiders as they were, how did the native Oneidas transform all the newcomers into dedicated Oneidas? It remains one of the great puzzles of American Indian history.

In the 17th and 18th centuries, Mohawks were by far the best known Iroquois. They overshadowed Oneidas to such an extent that some observers mistakenly referred to Oneidas as Mohawk "satellites." Oneidas were no one's satellites. They associated themselves with Onondaga or Mohawk positions, or acted on their own as best suited their interests. Yet 19th century histories went so far as to "explain" that Mohawks called Oneidas "children" because in the war with the Hurons and French in the 1640's

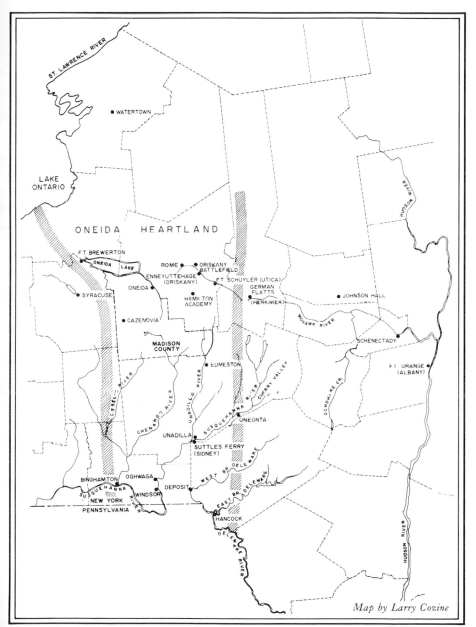

MAP 1. The Oneida Country, showing the location of places where events important in Oneida history occurred from the earliest European contacts to removal from New York.

Oneidas lost so many men that the Mohawks had to provide husbands for the widows to repopulate the village. This notion is based on a statement by Father Jacques Bruyas, a French Jesuit who lived with the Oneidas a generation after the war ended. It is only a myth. None of the contemporary Dutch documents mention such a defeat. Not even the French officials reported such a victory, although Jesuits lived with Hurons during the entire war and surely would have noticed such a significant triumph. Apparently Father Bruyas told the story to account for Mohawks addressing Oneidas as "children" in League councils. This form of address was part of League formality, expressing the parent-offspring, male-female duality that permeates all Iroquois social organization. It was not based on an historic incident any more than Iroquois reference to the English king as "father" was.

The same duality exists within the individual nations. Among the Oneidas, the dual principle associated the Tortoise with the Wolf clan on one side, leaving the Bear alone on the other. This duality often provides a basis for factionalism among the Iroquois nations even today.

The year 1649 did bring significant change in Oneida and Iroquois history. It saw the beginning of more profound alternations of all previously existing relationships between the different native American groups of the region. On March 16, a combined Iroquois strike-force took and destroyed two Huron towns, slaying Fathers Gabriel Lalemant and Jean

21

Brebeuf. As a result of this stunning defeat, the Hurons themselves abandoned and burned fifteen of their villages on May 1. Some 6,000 to 8,000 Hurons took refuge on Christian (St. Joseph) Island. Others dispersed to neighboring tribes. Members of one village even moved as a group into Oneida territory. All but a few hundred of the refugees on Christian Island died of starvation and disease in the frightful winter of 1649-50 and most of the survivors went to Quebec in the spring, where they founded the mission known as Lorette. Some of the rest joined the refugees among the Oneidas. In that same terrible winter of 1649-50, the main town of the Petuns, Huron neighbors, was destroyed while its warriors were away hunting the very Iroquois army that destroyed it. As a result, the Petuns, too, dispersed, following their Huron neighbors into exile.

Dispersion of Iroquoian speaking tribes that were not members of the League continued through 1650 and 1651 as the Neutrals, another related but independent nation, abandoned their homeland and either scattered into other areas or swelled the ranks of the victorious Iroquois.

These displaced peoples had a number of different effects upon the groups they joined. Displaced Hurons have been held responsible for attacks the Eries made on the Senecas in 1653. Others who joined the Iroquois ranks may have been at least partly responsible for the sudden peace moves by the Senecas, Cayugas, Onondagas and Oneidas. It is difficult to

22

explain the peace moves any other way. The Iroquois were winning the war. They had almost convinced the French authorities to abandon the frontier. Six years earlier, the Iroquois had killed Father Jogues, claiming he was a sorcerer who had cursed them with sickness and famine. Now they suddenly not only sought peace but also asked for missionaries. Hundreds of Christian Hurons, Petuns and Neutrals still strongly attracted to French co-religionists although refugees among the Oneidas and other members of the League seem to account for the abrupt policy switch.

The impact of the tremendous territorial dislocation of Iroquoian-speaking populations that took place between the first description of the Oneidas by Van den Bogaert in 1635 and the establishment of Christian missions there in 1656, only twenty-one years later, has never been adequately appreciated by historians. In less than a generation, several autonomous political entities with long prehistoric pasts disappeared, their populations scattered or absorbed by neighboring peoples. In 1657, Father Paul le Jeune, reporting from Onondaga, said that war and disease had depopulated that Nation so severely that foreigners outnumbered the natives. Peoples from seven different formerly independent Indian nations were settled there. The situation was the same throughout the Five Nations. More than eleven Nations were represented among the Seneca. In 1660, Father Hierosme Lalemont claimed that there were not more than 1,200 pure-blooded Iroquois left, both because of the high Iroquois mortality and the number of captive women who had been involved in the production of the generation of the 1660's. At this time, the Oneidas were said to have less than 100 warriors, a considerable drop in the twenty-five years since Van den Bogaert's visit. A conservative estimate based on the number of lodges that he saw would place the population of the main Oneida town alone as able to provide at least 200 warriors.

The Iroquois population suffered another severe blow from a smallpox epidemic that began in 1661 and continued through 1662. An example of its severity is provided by Father Hierosme Lalemant, who reported that 120 of 200 infants baptised during the winter had died. At the same time, Iroquois were under attack by their Susquehannock cousins from the south and Algonquian-speakers aided by Frenchmen on the north. New England Algonquian-speakers were also raiding.

In 1664, a significant change occured, although its consequences were not immediately apparent to the Iroquois. The Netherlands surrendered its colonial possessions in the New World to England. The Dutch merchants at Fort Orange, now named Albany, continued to operate unmolested for a time, however, so the actual change was so gradual the native Americans hardly noticed it. The Iroquois continued to call the new governors *Corlear* from the Dutch Van Curler, and treated them just as they had the Dutch leaders.

24

In 1668, Father Bruyas gave the first extensive description of Oneida life since Van den Bogaert's. By this time, he reported two-thirds of the Oneida villagers were former Huron and Algonquian captives. The native Oneidas could not have accomplished the massive feat of integrating this foreign majority without some cultural compromises, so the society Bruyas saw in 1668 should have been significantly different from the one Van den Bogaert saw in 1635. The two men were unfortunately interested in very different things so a point-by-point comparison is impossible.

Father Bruyas was particularly disturbed by the effects of alcohol on the people, something Van den Bogaert had not mentioned. It is difficult to say whether this was because the Oneidas did not drink so much in 1635 or Van den Bogaert did not think it worth mentioning. As stated above, these two observers had divergent ideas and what would seem important to one would be completely overlooked by the other.

Bruyas was also interested in Oneida family life, which Van den Bogaert totally ignored. The Jesuit called the Oneidas polygamous, but may have done so because they changed spouses easily and not because they had several at one time. He indicated a marriage usually broke up if the couple failed to have children. He knew of only one case in which this did not happen. Perhaps significantly, the husband in that marriage was a former captive, not a native-born Oneida.

Father Bruyas pointed out that Oneidas followed

25

"the law of the Jews," that is, they practiced the levirate. When a man died, his brother took his place in the marriage. The good father also provided another homely little detail about Oneida life. He said the women did hardly anything all winter but travel to bring in the meat of the deer or moose the man had killed. This pattern of a woman bringing in meat some man of her family killed is common among native Americans.

Father Bruyas also reported on the effects of the war with the Susquehannocks or *Andastogues*. In 1668, four Susquehannock female captives were burned to death at Oneida, and the Oneidas sent another male captive to the Mohawks to be burned. The next year, the Onondagas gave the Oneidas two Susquehannock captives, a young man and a woman, from nine they took during a raid. Given to replace an Oneida man slain by Susquehannocks, the woman was tortured for two days and nights before being killed because the man she replaced had suffered that fate at the Susquehannock village.

The Jesuit gives one of the earliest descriptions of Oneida raiding, reporting three alternative patterns. In one, individual Oneidas went out to sneak into a sleeping village, kill one or more enemies and escape with forty or fifty pursuers at their heels. This was regarded as an act of supreme prowess. In a second pattern, small groups of five to eight men went together. The final pattern involved a large mixed force. One Bruyas saw included 120 men — sixty Oneidas, fifty Onondagas and ten Cayugas.

26

In the only part of his report reminiscent of Van den Bogaert's description, Bruyas mentions a woman native religious leader who held dances, songs and feasts at her home every day. This suggests continuation of the female participation or leadership in religious ceremonies.

Even though he complained about Oneida licentiousness and drinking, Father Bruyas was impressed by their interest in learning. In 1669, he reported that the women were busy learning the catechism while the men were at war or hunting. To encourage them, he rewarded superior performance with strings of beads, little glass cylinders, or brass rings. The Iroquois custom for years had been to give gifts at speeches, and to validate the truthfulness or official nature of specific speeches with strings of wampum, so the distribution of these gifts, particularly the strings of beads, probably increased the significance of the performance to the women, who were not accustomed to speaking in public.

By 1672, the effects of Jesuit preaching began to show. Father Pierre Millet, who replaced Father Bruyas, reported that the traditional system of feasts and ceremonies was beginning to break down as Christians refused to participate. Depopulation was causing problems. He commented that men, who were providers of food and clothing, were scarce. Church services had begun to attract native Oneidas as well as former captives, so now praying in chorus was held in two languages, Huron and Oneida.

In 1673, Father Millet made the first statement

about Oneida "royalty," or at least what later writers seeking analogies with Europe persistently referred to as "royalty," "nobles" or "princesses." Millet simply called them "leaders." Each family, he said, had leaders called *Agoianderes* who were responsible for providing beads and collars to be used in negotiating with other Nations. Each family — probably the clan — met privately to collect beads from individual members and then the leaders showed in council what had been offered. A family/clan chief, either the eldest or one chosen for eloquence, spoke between songs. Each collar represented a deceased family member, according to Millet, and the families/clans took turns presenting their beads, one each day. Each was thanked and presented gifts in exchange for the beads. Finally, on the last day, all the collars were hung up in the council house and each was identified as to source and purpose. All of the collars were placed together and the full Oneida council of elders decided how many would be sent to whom, and what matters would be negotiated.

This description does not sound like anything seen by Van den Bogaert. Possibly Father Millet observed the sort of activity Van den Bogaert did not observe that went on in another house before he and the Oneidas counseled with the Onondagas. The purpose of the council observed by Millet was different from the aims of those observed by Van den Bogaert, which may have been a factor. Council meetings might well have altered drastically in the intervening years. Parts of the council Millet described remark-

28

ably resemble a modern "condolence" ceremony among the New York and Canadian Iroquois, held to install new chiefs to replace those who have died.

The entrance of ambassadors or negotiators as described by Millet, was a ceremonious affair. The negotiating party stopped within musket shot of the settlement and waited for local elders to emerge to meet them. After proper identification and ritual greeting exchange, the ambassadors were escorted by the elders and others of the community into the settlement where a special cabin was set aside for them. Everyone in the village gave them food and presents — this had not changed since 1635. The young men hunted to provide food for the visitors. Then negotiations went forward in a four-day ceremony with propositions presented, discussed, and responded to by the hosts. The four-day ritual may have been new. Van den Bogaert had only one or at the most two-day councils.

The Iroquois-Susquehannock war finally ended in 1675. Settlers in Pennsylvania unwittingly helped the Iroquois by constant attacks on the Susquehannocks who ultimately dispersed like many other tribes. Most of them moved into Seneca territory to be incorporated into that nation, but others moved south and west to disappear from historical notice. Some joined the new detribalized bands beginning to settle in the dangerous fringe area between encroaching white settlements and established tribal territories. These unaffiliated peoples became more and more of a menace to both colonial and native

Americans as time passed. They were claimed by no one and controlled by no one. Yet, because individuals came from many different tribes, their raids were blamed on almost every tribe — usually the most convenient target from the colonial American's point of view.

Christian missions continued to prosper in the Iroquois heartland. A major Oneida chief, *Soenrese*, converted and was baptized on January 1, 1676, encouraging many others to follow his example. That same year, *Kryn*, a Mohawk chief led at least 40 followers to St. Xavier des Pres. Thus it became known as a Mohawk rather than an Oneida mission. French officials moved it, and changed its name to St. Francois Cavier du Sault, but to Englishmen and Six Nations alike it was known as *Caughnawaga*. Actually it was no more Mohawk than it had been Oneida. The Jesuits reported that ten to twelve Iroquoian-speaking nations were represented there. Later, remnants of even more groups drifted into the station.

At a council meeting in New York in 1679, the Five Nations granted New York colony sovereignty over their Susquehannock lands. Thus began the major land cessions that continued for over 100 years until the Iroquois had only a fraction of their homeland left. At this 1679 council, an Oneida speaker announced that his fellow tribesmen were subjects of *Corlear*. He also said that *Corlear* "governed the whole land from New York to Albany and from there to the Sennekas land." Considering that as late as 1678 the Oneidas were referred to in documents as one of the "Sinnekens" or "Sineques," this was not nearly the concession that later historians made it out to be. It was probably meant as no more than diplomatic talk. The Iroquois were trying at the time to win English assistance against French attack, and invoked their protection as subjects to do so.

A general problem in all councils and treaties is that there is no way of knowing whether Indians said what the interpreters reported, or whether they were honestly told what they were signing. There is evidence from later treaty negotiations that interpreters were bribed and Indians, therefore, undoubtedly sometimes signed documents that said things quite different from what they thought was in them, at least until they could read and understand treaties themselves. In any case, the "land cession" of 1679 was hardly held to be such except by people in New York who were concerned with keeping people in Pennsylvania from gaining control over the area evacuated by the Susquehannock Indians. It did mark the beginning of intensive colonial interest in acquiring title to large areas of Indian land.

Another treaty in 1683 confirmed English rights to all former Susquehannock territory above Wyalusing. During these negotiations, which apparently were taken more seriously by the Iroquois, the Cayuga and Onondaga argued that no one had any right to do anything about this particular land but

31

themselves. This position foreshadowed later land deals by individual Nations that cost the Iroquois much territory later.

In 1682, the total Five Nations population was estimated at 13,000. Many of those counted were "naturalized" Iroquois, captives or voluntary recruits, but the figure is one of the highest in the 1600's. It would never be that high again. The 1680's also marked the end of a truly independent Five Nations League. In 1684, in council at Onondaga, the Five Nations chief announced that they were brothers, not vassals of the English king. In 1688, after a sharp defeat inflicted by a French invasion force in Seneca country, the Oneidas, Onondagas and Cayugas declared themselves neutral. From then on, Five Nations policy tended to reflect more closely alliances with particular countries and to parallel European events.

After 1690, English officials began to grant individuals permission to purchase Indian land. That right had been almost exclusively reserved to the government. Land conflicts, as well as white pressure on the land, immediately began to increase.

The Five Nations were not able to keep their neutral position in the struggle between France and England. The conflict went on, and the Oneidas got Father Millet back in 1691 as a prisoner after he left in 1684 because of the deteriorating French position. The Onondagas wanted to execute him as a war criminal. The Oneida council decided to give him to replace *Otassete,* a chief who died of disease, not in battle, so Millet's life was spared. What made matters even worse from the English point of view was that *Otassete* had been a council member and Father Millet was not only allowed but required to attend council meetings and to vote as the chief's replacement. Some of the more astute Oneida council members used Millet to find out what the English colonials were really up to, or to speak harshly to English representatives when the Oneidas were annoyed but did not want to risk an open breach with the Englishmen. This position may have given Father Millet, and through him France, a considerable advantage, but it was quite useful to the Oneidas.

The Oneidas suffered a terrible year in 1692. Not only were they still losing people to smallpox, but a battle with the French just outside Montreal was disastrous. Surprised inside a house, almost all of the Oneida warriors, including many of their principal chiefs, were killed. A factor that made this loss even more bitter to Oneidas was the presence in the French forces of a Cayuga chief and several Caughnawaga Iroquois.

Oneidas and others of the Five Nations continued to make up their losses with prisoners until by 1694 Onondagas said that almost half of their chieftainships were in the hands of Frenchmen while at least two (Father Miller and one other) participated in general League councils as part of the Oneida delegation. It is not surprising that the Five Nations sought peace. The amazing thing is that they kept up the combat so long. France did so well in this war that in 1695 Louis XIV discontinued the reward of ten silver *ecus* for dead Iroquois and twenty for every male prisoner, on the grounds that it was too expensive.

A thousand Frenchmen and as many Indians invaded Iroquois territory in 1696, attacking an Onondaga village whose inhabitants burned it and fled. Oneidas sent messengers to the French forces to ask for peace. The messengers arrived just as the Frenchmen were destroying Onondaga food supplies. Frontenac, the commander, agreed to peace only if all the Oneidas would move to Canada. He must have assumed they would never agree or it was too late to recall his forces, for while negotiations were still going on, 700 men under de Vaudreuil attacked Oneida, burned the village, cut down the growing maize and took several prisoners, one of whom was later burned at Montreal. Official documents blamed the Algonquians for his death, but the Jesuit Lamberville, who recognized the Oneida as a benevolent and devout man always friendly to the French cause, claimed colonial officials could have saved him. The Treaty of Ryswick that ended King William's War in 1697 could not remove the bitterness engendered by such wartime actions.

The Oneida emissaries to Frontenac actually agreed to move to Canada. After the destruction of their village, however, only thirty-three went and these were those most in favor of the Frenchmen. By the time of the treaty, Iroquois war strength had

34

dropped from 2,550 to 1,230. Some of the loss was due to defections to Canada, but the bulk resulted from smallpox and warfare. Oneida numbers had fallen from 180 warriors to only seventy. In their search for peace, Oneidas suggested a solution that was adopted in modified form a century and a half later. They sought Canadian land for a new settlement where the Oneida name might be preserved. Onondagas and Mohawks objected, however, and the idea was dropped. When they moved to Wisconsin, the Oneidas succeeded in accomplishing something they first attempted in 1697 — obtaining land where they could preserve their Oneida identity.

Iroquois affairs continued along much the same pattern through the first half of the 18th century. The frequency of raids fell in the colonies when Europe was at peace, although there was almost always a skirmish or two somewhere. When fighting broke out between France and England, the intensity of conflict increased in the New World.

The period of 1711-12 proved to be an important one for the Oneidas, although the events that occurred then did not bring immediately significant consequences. In 1711, the Tuscaroras, an Iroquoian group living in the Carolinas, went to war against Englishmen, killing 130 colonists in one day. The colonials did not bear their burden patiently. Aided by other southern native Americans, they took the main Tuscarora town by force in 1713 and sold 800 Tuscarora captives into slavery. The rest were allowed to ask the New York Iroquois for permission to settle in their territory. At a council in Albany on September 20, 1714, the Tuscaroras were offered a site in what is now Madison County, New York, north and west of the Chenango River in the border area between Oneida and Onondaga heartlands. The Tuscaroras moved slowly into their new lands and in 1722 they took their place at an Albany council as full League members. From 1722 on, the Iroquois League was known as the Six Nations.

A second event in 1712 also held implications for the future. An English Protestant mission to the Oneidas brought them William Andrews to teach school for three years. As a missionary, he set a new tone. Instead of being impressed like the Jesuits with Oneida courage, industry and piety, Andrews regarded Oneidas as sordid, mercenary, beggerly people who would never be anything but pagan. Unfortunately, this attitude was shared by many ministers and teachers who followed him. Consequently, missionaries who were sincerely devoted to Oneida interests and respected the Oneidas as people had continually to battle with those who denigrated them. Men hostile toward Oneidas often had access to the press and the pulpit and helped to create a climate of prejudice and misunderstanding about them that persists to this day.

The Tuscaroras provide the sole example of successful amalgamation to full membership in the League, but they were only one of a number of different groups attempting to join. Although many of these were tentatively admitted at various times, or

36

were figuratively allowed to shelter under the great tree, none of the others ever achieved full League membership. The many attempts reflected the continued disruption of native American life and the increasingly rapid disappearance of previously independent peoples from areas now swarming with European and American-born colonists — a situation that made the relative stability of the Iroquois even more noticeable and attractive.

The Iroquois were stable only by comparison. Disruption afflicted them, too. Not only did they absorb a host of new people all the time, but they also steadily lost cohesiveness and personnel. Having begun to disperse through defections to Canada in the 1600's, the Oneidas began scattering southward in the early 1700's. The community of *Oghwaga* near present Windsor, New York, in southern Oneida territory, was becoming an important center. Although it was originally an Oneida town, it attracted refugees from many nations. By 1746 references to the Oghwagans were made as if they were a separate people. They had their own leaders, and made their own decisions independently from the Oneida council that met in the traditional center.

Partly because of this southern movement and also because of increasing problems with the colonists on the Susquehanna, the League named an Oneida called *Qugquaterughiathe* or *Swatana* to move to Pennsylvania to keep an eye on the activities there. Better known by his Delaware name *Shikellimy*, he played a very important role in the complex relationships between the colonists, Iroquois, Shawnees and Delawares. In 1732, he and Conrad Weiser were appointed agents between the Six Nations and Pennsylvania colony.

Some Oneidas were moving west as well as south. By 1748, some 434 Iroquois warriors, including fifteen Oneidas, were reported living probably with their families on the Ohio River. In 1750, Governor Hamilton complained that there were more Six Nations people living on the branches of the Mississippi than remained in New York. Thus, long before any official talk of removal, pioneer Oneidas were already moving to establish new homes to the west.

These new groupings, a combination of Six Nations members, Shawnees, Hurons, Delawares and others, could field some 1,500 to 2,000 warriors. Because they felt no allegiance to any established nation, they created a great deal of anxiety in the colonies.

Wars and raiding continued, but Iroquois alliances and enmities shifted. The Shawnees, who received asylum and fought as allies a few years earlier, came under French influence as they migrated westward and became bitter enemies by the 1730's. Catawbas and Cherokees far to the south became new enemies, probably reflecting Iroquois incorporation of Tuscarora quarrels along with the Tuscarora.

Disease continued taking a heavy toll. Smallpox was probably the worst killer. An epidemic struck in 1736 and did not peak until 1739 when the annual

38

council had to be cancelled. Another epidemic came in 1746 and caused delays in projected raids on the French border. Ten years later in 1756, smallpox was again a problem and added its toll to the cost of the French and Indian War. A frightful epidemic in 1780 took uncounted numbers of lives, not only among the Iroquois in New York colony, but throughout America.

Pressure on Iroquois land continued to mount, and League territory and power continued to erode. At the same time, some colonials increased their predatory incursions, but others tried to ease the adjustment problems and provide native Americans with skills needed to cope with a changing world. A variety of individuals, many of them churchmen, opened schools and academies for the instruction of native American youths. Some of these provided the best or even the only formal education available to anyone on the frontier. Consequently, they were as well attended by colonials as by native Americans. Oneidas, along with other peoples, were becoming literate English speakers, and consequently less dependent on foreign interpreters.

New nations continually joined the parade of displaced people. In 1748, the Catawbas, who had been fighting the Six Nations since early in the century, allied with them and attended councils, although they could not vote. Nanticokes from New England had much the same status. They eventually formed one of the components that went to make up the Brotherton Indians.

Another significant event in the history of the Oneidas took place in 1750 when Sir William Johnson took up his duties as Superintendent of Indian Affairs. For the next generation he had more influence on Six Nations activities than anyone else. His relationships with the Iroquois were extraordinarily good for all that period.

One of Johnson's early actions was to begin trading for ginseng, lending his support to a form of trade that was to remain popular for generations. Johnson also took more interest in native American customs than most of his predecessors had. He commented, for example, on the fact that messages to the Six Nations had to be accompanied or confirmed by a string or belt of wampum if they were to be believed. Without this, they might be ignored or rejected. Many observers had pointed out that Iroquois had the "custom" of giving strings, belts or collars of beads, but no one had previously mentioned the validating functions of these gifts. His attention to detail may be one of the reasons Johnson had a profound influence. He understood the nuances of Iroquois culture better than any European had before. He did not dismiss native American behavior as simply "quaint" or "savage." He cared about it and thought it was worth understanding.

The French and Indian War provided Sir William with his first test, a severe one. He competed with the French agent Duquesne, who had almost won over the Oneidas, Cayugas and Tuscaroras. In addition, the behavior of British generals toward native

Americans was a serious handicap to Johnson. Braddock's 1755 defeat almost drove the Iroquois into the arms of France both because it raised doubts as to the ability of England to protect them, and because the stupidity and arrogance of English generals disgusted them. *Scarrooyada*, an Oneida who had succeeded the Half King as head of the Oghwaga people, reported that although he had been available to Braddock all the time, the General never once consulted him and would not even listen to him. Yet the battle took place on terrain *Scarrooyada* knew and was fought by methods in which he was expert.

French influence became so strong at Oneida and Onondaga after the battle that *Scarrooyada* suggested that Englishmen interested in business with Iroquois would do well to avoid those places. In July, eighty Oneidas and Onondagas went to New France as a peace delegation. French officials stupidly imprisoned them and held them hostage. This seemed effective in the short range situation. In December, the Oneidas turned over to French officials the medals the Britishers had given them and sent the Cayugas a wampum belt with an English scalp attached, suggesting they join the Frenchmen. The English cause never appeared so near being lost.

So sure were the French representatives that they had won Oneida loyalty that they informed the Oneida lake village of an impending attack on German Flats. The fact that the Oneidas promptly warned the settlers indicates that French judgment was somewhat inaccurate.

41

Actually the Oneidas were split as usual between English and French supporters. By 1759, the people who favored England had greatly improved their position, due primarily to the steady work of Sir William Johnson. Forts had been promised and constructed: Royal Blockhouse at the head of Oneida Lake and Fort Brewerton at the foot. Oneida sentiment had so changed that Oneidas advised the Nanticokes to return a French hatchet sent to encourage them to war against England.

In the next year, Johnson was able to raise 1,330 warriors to agree to go with him against the French. Sixty were Oneidas. Then 1760 saw the ultimate defeat of the French colonial forces by British armies and peace was finally established on the northern Iroquois frontier.

Peace, after so many generations of war, did not eliminate the threat to Oneida survival. It merely changed the nature of the threat. 1761 saw an upsurge in missionary activity that was not to die down for over 100 years. Several missionaries were native Americans. David Fowler, a Montauk, had an indirect influence out of proportion to the length of his visit. At the time, he simply selected three Iroquois to go back to Boston for an education. Later, he was instrumental in persuading Oneidas to give a tract of land 12 miles square some 14 miles south of present Utica, New York, for a collection of New England and Long Island tribes which became known as the Brotherton Indians.

Another missionary who was to have a profound

and direct influence on Oneida life paid his first visit in 1761, accompanied by Joseph Brant. Samuel Kirkland did not stay long on this visit, but five years later returned to take up a post he continued to hold for forty years through some of the most difficult times the Oneidas had yet faced. Without his presence and influence, Oneida history would certainly have been different in many ways.

Peace with the French did not remove all causes for war, and Pontiac's War began in 1763. This was a true "Indian" war. For what was probably the first time native Americans — Delawares, the Ottawa confederacy and others — joined together to drive the white man from the land. It may have been one of the earliest situations when battle lines were clearly drawn between native Americans and European invaders.

Many native Americans were disillusioned with colonists, disgusted with their greed for land, their arrogance and intolerance. Even clergymen were often justly suspected of having more hunger for land than for saving souls. The disillusioned were some of the people who joined Pontiac. Other native Americans had gone too far along the path of cultural change to be willing or able to turn back. Iroquois, by this time, were heavily dependent on trade goods for survival. The use of the bow and arrow had seriously declined even for hunting. Iron cooking kettles were no longer luxuries, but necessities. Gunpowder and lead to supply the guns that had replaced bows and arrows were even more clearly essential supplies. A man went out on his main provisioning hunting trips twice a year, and to get through these two seasons, he needed eight pounds of powder and twenty pounds of lead. Less and he would not be able to supply the meat he needed to last himself and his family through the year. Maize and other staples were important, but they were not enough.

Indian dependence on colonial sources of supply provided Sir William Johnson with a powerful lever. The Iroquois were not short-sighted, and they had made their decision some years before. When Johnson sent the war belt to the Oneidas and Tuscaroras, they were not hesitant. Most of the fighting was against the Delaware to the south and west so Oghwaga became the main base of operations. Iroquois success led to the Delawares abandoning their easternmost towns and heading farther west.

When the war broke out, the Oneidas had two main villages, one about twenty-five miles from Fort Stanwix and the other twelve miles from Oneida Lake. In addition, individual families were scattered in several small settlements and outlying cabins south toward the Susquehanna River. These dispersed settlements collectively could raise 250 warriors. Intermingled with the Oneidas were Tuscaroras who had several small settlements along the Susquehanna and one main village six miles from Oneida, which could field 140 warriors. Oghwaga, still regarded by many as an Oneida town, was the

A PORTRAIT of the Reverend Samuel Kirkland, missionary to the Oneida Nation and founder of Hamilton Academy.

largest settlement in the southern New York area. It had fifteen to sixteen big houses on the east side of the river with a smaller "suburb" on the west side and could provide about 140 warriors. A Tuscarora town three miles downstream had about the same number of people. The two communities shared the spring shad fishing which was better at the Tuscarora site. The houses of both settlements were scattered, not tightly clustered around a village common, nor were the communities palisaded as earlier villages had been.

In 1768, the treaty of Fort Stanwix involved the Oneidas in a major land cession. Missionaries in the area were almost all opposed to the treaty because it involved so much of Oneida heartland. Sir William Johnson outmaneuvered them by pointing out to the Six Nations delegates that the missionaries were from New England and suggested that they were probably after the Susquehanna lands themselves. Native Americans had long been aware of the rivalry between the various colonies over control of Susquehanna lands, so this suggestion seemed plausible and bore fruit. The Oneidas, headed by *Conogh-quieson*, signed the treaty along with the rest, thereby opening land south and east of the Ohio, Susquehanna and Unadilla Rivers to colonial settlement. The treaty did reserve the land immediately around any Iroquois settlements that happened to be in the ceded area. It involved land in Kentucky and West Virginia as well as New York and Pennsylvania, although Iroquois sovereignty over those lands was disputed by various other native American nations, especially the Delaware.

After the land cession, matters were relatively quiet for a few years. Tension grew between mother country and colonists and between colonists and native Americans. For example, several members of Shikellimy's family were murdered, probably by a colonist band. Sir William Johnson died suddenly in 1774 after a rather emotional council meeting. There was then no one who had the widespread overall influence that Johnson had exercised. Joseph and Molly Brant were strongly pro-British, but their influence was most powerful among the Mohawks. Samuel Kirkland was in favor of the colonists, and his influence was limited to the Oneidas, particularly their Christian faction.

The Provincial Congress asked Kirkland to help in at least keeping the Oneidas out of the Revolutionary War on the British side. He did his best. He aroused Oneida indignation by telling them, among other things, that inasmuch as the king would not allow goods to be sent either to the colonies or to the Indians, powder and other items would soon be very expensive. Tories, on the other hand, sent word through the Six Nations to look to King George as their true protector and to shun evil advice. Col. Guy Johnson, who succeeded Sir William, managed to force Kirkland to move to Cherry Valley and prohibited him from having any contact with Oneidas until after the Provincial Congress closed. Both sides did their best to gain Iroquois support.

In August of 1775, at the last council ever held in Albany between the Six Nations and English officials, members of the League could not agree on a course of action. The council fire of the League of the Iroquois was extinguished. Every nation could act on its own — forever, according to some historians. Actually, it was just for the duration of the Revolutionary War.

The Oneidas, like all other members of the League, were seriously divided by the question of the colonial revolt. One Oneida faction, including the war chief Skenandoah, supported Rev. Kirkland and the colonial rebels. This faction won out in the northern part of Oneida territory, and the Oneida council sent a message to Governor Trumbull of Connecticut in which it welcomed the Stockbridge Indians, who had just settled in their country, and assured the Governor that Oneidas intended to stay neutral in the conflict.

The people at Oghwaga, however, did not go along with the Oneida council decision. Oghwaga became a major base for the Mohawk Brant and his adherents. Oneidas who did not sympathize with England were forced from their homes, not only at Oghwaga, but throughout the Oneida heartland.

At first, the Oneidas assumed that other members of the League would accept and respect their position of neutrality. They did not intend to engage in any fraticidal war. Perhaps the other League members did intend to respect Oneida neutrality, but the battle at Oriskany in 1777 changed everything. In June of that year, General Herkimer tried to head off a confrontation between colonials, Iroquois factions and Englishmen by holding a council with Brant at Unadilla. The conference broke down without any improvement in the situation. By June 29, raids were being made up and down the Unadilla valley and all along the frontier. Based at Oghwaga with at least 700 warriors, Brant used his knowledge of the area to good effect.

Factional divisions among the separate Six Nations were a problem to both sides. No one could be sure where loyalties lay for any given individual. Thomas Spencer, an Oneida, took part in an English council at St. Regis where an attack on Fort Stanwix was planned. He promptly informed the colonials. When General Herkimer started to lead his troops into battle, Spencer warned him that an ambush was prepared for him at Oriskany. Herkimer pressed ahead when his officers accused him of cowardice. Soon the revolutionary colonists, Oneidas and Tuscaroras with him were fighting for their lives. Onondagas, Senecas and Cayugas who had been invited along as observers also found themselves caught up in the fighting. The Onondagas alone lost ninety, three of them chiefs. The colonists lost over 200 men, but would have lost many more without the courageous fighting of their native American allies.

THE ONEIDA CHIEF SKENANDOAH. Whether this portrait depicts the Revolutionary War Oneida Leader, or his War of 1812 — Oneida Removal period namesake is uncertain.

Oriskany set Oneidas and Tuscaroras against the rest of the Six Nations. Oneida villages were no longer thought of as neutral. Loyalists burned Oneida houses, destroyed crops and stole cattle. Oneidas retaliated, first by attacking a Tory mill at Edmeston. Then, joining with Tuscaroras, the Oneidas swept through the Unadilla Valley, took prisoners and recaptured some of their cattle. This pattern of raid and retaliation continued throughout the war with the result that almost all non-combatants left for safer parts.

In 1779, the colonials sent a force led by Gen. Sullivan to attack the Iroquois homelands. Rev. Samuel Kirkland served as Brigade Chaplain, and Oneidas served both as guides and as officers.

This Oneida participation enraged other members of the League. Their raids or threats became so great that the majority of the Oneidas moved to the neighborhood of Schenectady for the duration of the war. Some, following the old pattern, joined the enemy. Col. Guy Johnson said that over 330 Oneidas — a number that later swelled to 800 — including women and children, had joined him.

The Oneidas themselves were safe, but their village, their church, and their colonial-style houses were burned. As a result of the war, the Oneidas lost everything it had taken them years to build, and they had to start all over.

Sullivan's raid destroyed a huge number of crops and fruit orchards. Peaches had been particularly popular among the Six Nations, and thousands of trees were cut down. Still, Sullivan's raid did not have the devastating effect on Iroquois fighting forces that historians have claimed for it. Instead of defeating the Six Nations, the raid simply confirmed the invaded nations in their conviction that their cause was just and that they were entitled to revenge.

Six Nations warriors ravaged the Schoharie and Mohawk Valleys the year after Sullivan's raid, and repeated the same process in 1781 just to prove the first retaliation was no accident. Their fighting prowess did not seem to have been seriously impaired.

Oneidas played a vital role on the colonial side during the Revolution, despite factional disputes. Because of their ability to join enemy councils freely, Oneidas were an invaluable source of information to the revolutionaries. According to some historians, it was the Oneida chief Skenandoah who killed Walter Butler, notorious for leading the British force that massacred settlers in Cherry Valley, during a skirmish in 1781. Oneida tradition speaks of Polly Cooper serving as a cook without pay for General George Washington throughout the war. At the end of hostilities, a grateful Martha Washington presented her with a shawl. It was Oneida maize delivered at a crucial time that enabled Washington and his troops to survive the terrible winter at Valley Forge. In addition to their own raids down the Unadilla Valley, Oneida warriors fought alongside colonial soldiers, serving as scouts and guides. The Oneida garrison at Palmer's Falls on the

Hudson was the only one north of the Mohawk Valley.

Oneidas intervened to save the young French Marquis de Lafayette when he rashly moved his forces into a difficult position at Barren Hill.

Although the contemporary colonials recognized the decisive nature of Oneida and Tuscacora intervention in the Revolutionary War, subsequent historians tended to overlook their contribution. Popular writers of the 19th century made villains of the Mohawks, and heroes of Mohicans or Delawares, both traditional enemies of the Iroquois. They ignored Oneida and Tuscacora heroes.

With the American Revolution ended, a treaty was signed at Fort Stanwix in 1784. This agreement confirmed Oneida and Tuscarora ownership of their lands, but forced the rest of the Six Nations to give up most of their territory. New York State awarded Rev. Samuel Kirkland 4,000 acres of land near Fort Schuyler (not Utica) in appreciation for his services to the American cause during the war. Kirkland used most of this land to found Oneida Academy for the education of Oneida young men and women. The quality of education at Oneida Academy was so high for that area and time that colonial as well as native Americans always attended it. When it later became Hamilton College, Oneida attendance declined, partly because the Oneida moved west. It was also closed to women, thus completely changing its character.

The last phase of Oneida land ownership in New

York State began in 1788. The state paid $11,500 to the Oneidas and Tuscaroras jointly, plus an additional $5,500 to the Oneidas alone, and promised the latter a $600 annuity "forever" for title to the remainder of their land in New York except for the areas immediately around their villages which they reserved. The next year, New York State gained jurisdiction over criminal affairs among the Oneidas by a treaty negotiated at Fort Herkimer. This made the native Americans of New York essentially an interior dependent nation. The Oneidas never again regarded armed force as a feasible means for solving differences between them and other Americans.

In 1792, the Catskill-Susquehanna Road which had been opened in 1769 was widened to twenty-five feet. Herds of cattle and sheep began traveling along it and a regular weekly mail route was established. The Oneida area was losing its frontier character. There were only 630 Oneidas left in New York at that time. Six miles from the largest Oneida settlement lived 280 Stockbridges, while 250 Brothertons lived twenty miles away. Thus, forty-six percent of the 1,160 native Americans living on Oneida land were not Oneidas.

White pressure on the land constantly became more intense. The same year the Catskill-Susquehanna Road was widened, the Holland Land Company purchased 1,000,000 acres of land and took options on 800,000 acres more from Robert Morris on condition that Indian title be extinguished. Naturally enough, Morris sought to do everything he could to complete his bargain. Everywhere along the frontier, settlers, many of them poor and irresponsible, purchased or squatted on former Iroquois lands, demanding roads, mills, markets, schools and other conveniences from the land developers or the government. To most of these people, native Americans were heathen nuisances. They saw nothing good in the native American way of life and felt that the only reasonable choices for the native Americans were to live like white people, to move west beyond the reach of "civilization," or to "disappear" in some convenient way — preferably with a minimum of fuss. That was at least the attitude of the well-intentioned whites. The unscrupulous ones regarded the native American as fair game and legitimate prey, and went even beyond the normal sharp practices of the day when cheating by both buyers and sellers was regarded as good business. The frequency of outright robbery led well-meaning people to sponsor laws intended to protect native Americans not only from the scoundrels, but also from themselves. Such laws rarely worked. It was difficult to enforce them, or to convict those accused under them, and victims themselves often conspired to thwart law officers.

The Big Tree land treaty in 1797 illustrates both the need for and the futility of such laws. Robert Morris instigated the treaty council to complete his bargain with the Holland Land Company. There was still Iroquois opposition to any more land sales. Opponents pointed to the Oneidas as a horrible example of their consequences. The Oneidas were richer since they had sold out to New York State, but they had lost influence among the Six Nations. In fact, some Iroquois hardly regarded the Oneidas as members of the League. Yet, Morris and the land company agents were determined. Records of the Holland Land Company show how they persuaded Iroquois to sign the treaty. Morris divided $4,000 among the three interpreters, and subsequently gave them another $1,000 each. He gave $5,000 to the agent of the federal government. Chiefs also collected handsomely. Red Jacket and Cornplanter obtained the most money. The records show that Red Jacket was paid $600 in cash and an annuity of $100 annually for life. Cornplanter received $300 in cash and a $200 annuity which was continued to his heirs after his death.

The beginning of the 19th century found the Iroquois living in a very different situation from the pre-revolutionary one. The League had been split and the council fire extinguished. The major portion of the League had been defeated in battle, and retained what little land each Nation held only through the generosity of the winners. Although the Oneidas had fought on the winning side and had been confirmed in their land holdings, they were no better off than the losers because they had promptly sold all their land to New York State. Settlers were pouring into what had been exclusively native American lands. When Samuel Kirkland died in 1808, the Oneidas lost a major link to the non-Iroquois world.

In 1810, the Holland Land Company sold its pre-emptive rights to David A. Ogden for fifty cents per acre, opening the way for the next major push to move the Iroquois out of New York.

The War of 1812 brought no major changes to the Oneida condition. The Canadian Iroquois again took up arms against the United States. The United States Iroquois declared war on Canada, yet actual Iroquois involvement in battle was minor compared with previous conflicts.

The year 1817 proved decisive for the 1,500 Oneidas in New York. Episcopal Bishop John H. Hobart appointed Eleazer Williams as a Lay Reader to the Oneidas at his own request. Williams was a Mohawk, one of whose ancestors was said to be the captive, Eunice Williams. He became an extraordinarily controversial figure, sometimes reputed to be the "Lost Dauphin" of France. Charges and counter-charges swirled around him from both colonial and native American sources. He was hailed as a protector and far-sighted dedicated leader, or denounced as a scoundrel seeking power and profit at the expense of deluded Oneidas. Evaluation of Williams depends partly on whether the Oneida move to Wisconsin is judged to be good or bad, inasmuch as he was certainly a prime factor in bringing it about.

When he arrived at Oneida, Williams found two major divisions, the First Christian Party and the so-called pagans. He almost at once converted the Pagan Party. In 1817, this group accompanied Williams to Albany to donate a bit of remaining land for a church and a fund to support a minister. These Oneidas asked to be called the Second-Christian Party and went on to build a church thirty-six feet by fifty feet with a small tower.

At this same time, several different forces began to converge toward removal of New York Oneidas to the west. David Ogden saw removal of all the Six Nations, not just the Oneidas, as a solution to clearing his title to Iroquois lands. Samuel U. Hendrick, chief of the Stockbridges, saw removal as a way to escape non-Indian pressures and to find more room for his people. The Seneca missionary Rev. John Sergeant had much the same idea. The American Board of Missions agreed and appointed Jedediah Morse to go look for suitable land. John Metoxen, a Stockbridge, did not wait for official action. He moved his whole family, in company with one other, to Miami Indian land on the White River. The Miamis had confirmed this land cession to the Stockbridges in July of 1817. Yet, after Metoxen's group had moved to it, the Miamis sold out to the United States, leaving the Stockbridges stranded.

Eleazer Williams began to promote the idea of an Indian Confederacy uniting all native American tribes into a union located somewhere in the west. He persuaded four or five young chiefs among the Oneida to join him, and in 1818 they began communications with the War Department while they intensified efforts to build more support for the idea within the Six Nations. Lines of factional cleavage deepened at once as opposition to removal burgeoned as rapidly as support.

According to the reports of Bishop Hobart and Jasper Parrish, the Oneidas were by this time no longer "savage." Reservation land was held by the Nation as a whole. On it individual Oneidas grew tobacco, potatoes, maize, beans and pumpkins or raised sheep and cows. They lived in bark or log houses scattered throughout the reserved land, rather then concentrated in a single center. Ginseng continued to be a major source of cash income. Oneidas gathered about 1,000 bushels a year, realizing an average of $2,000 from its sale. A few Oneidas were literate, but the majority spoke only Oneida and could not write either English or their own language.

Eleazer Williams arrived at Detroit late in July of 1820 with a group of Oneidas and Stockbridges, expecting fulfillment of War Department promises for supplies and transport to Green Bay. They had to return home disappointed because of bureaucratic confusion. They returned again the next year. This time seven representatives from the other Six Nations had been added to the delegation besides Williams, three Stockbridges and four Oneidas. They reached the Winnebagoes and Menominees at Green Bay, where they managed to sign a treaty over the objections of the local French and mixed French-native American population. The amount of Wisconsin land obtained in this treaty was not nearly as much as the New York group wanted. Conse-

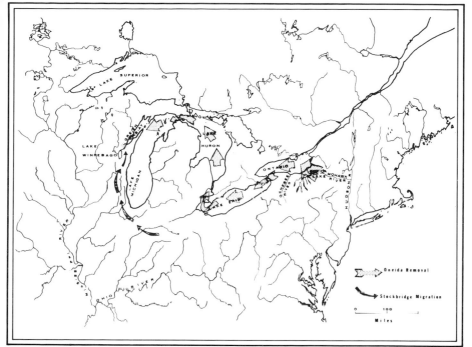

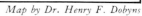

Map by Dr. Henry F. Dobyns

MAP 2. Oneida Removal from New York to Wisconsin, from an aboriginal homeland south of Lake Ontario to former Menominee lands west of Lake Michigan.

quently, when the delegation returned the next year with $1,500 worth of goods to pay for the 1821 cession, it reopened negotiations to try to obtain more land.

John Metoxen and his group of fifty Stockbridges, whose Miami land had been sold out from under them, took advantage of the 1821 cession and moved to Wisconsin. In the late fall of 1822, they settled on the east side of the Grand Kakalin confluence with the Fox River.

All this activity had stirred up strong opposition back in New York. The Oneida council condemned Williams and the young chiefs, repudiated the 1821 agreement, and expressed the firm decision to remain in the ancestral homeland. The issue also split the other Six Nations with the exception of the Senecas, who remained united in opposition to removal.

In spite of the Oneida council decision, Williams and his followers opened the 1822 negotiations and succeeded in obtaining an amazing concession from the Menominees. For goods worth $1,000 paid immediately and an equal amount due in 1823 and another equal quantity due in 1824, the Menominees granted the Oneidas a "right in common" to all their lands. When President Monroe signed this 1822 treaty, he limited the amount granted to the Oneidas, but the agreement was still an astonishing concession and one that was quickly challenged.

The Oneidas did not wait for the resolution of the conflict. In 1823, a sizeable band led by Eleazer

Williams and Chief Skenandoah — a descendent of the famous chief of Revolutionary War times — moved to Wisconsin. A group of Munsees, Mohicans, and Brothertons also moved and settled on the east side of the Fox River confluence with the Little Kakalin where they were joined by a small Oneida band led by Ned Atsiquet. This whole group moved in 1825 to Duck Creek, where the main Oneida settlement developed.

The Oneidas immediately built longhouses, and the women planted the fields to maize, beans and potatoes while the men hunted deer, turkey and duck or fished. Bands of Oneidas continued to move to Wisconsin, but the other members of the Six Nations remained adamant and refused to leave New York.

Opposition to the land cession kept growing among the Menominee Indians, helped along by their agent, Col. Samuel C. Stambaugh. It culminated in the total repudiation of the 1822 treaty by Oshkosh, the Menominee chief appointed by Governor Lewis Cass in 1827. The quarrel was taken to Washington in 1831, where the Menominee swore that they had never sold their land, or received anything from the Six Nations for it.

Plans for the Menominee Washington trip leaked out to the Oneidas. Much against Col. Stambaugh's wishes, therefore, Chief Daniel Bread and Eleazer Williams along with two men appointed by Gov. Cass accompanied the Menominee delegation to Washington. All the protests of this group could do

64

CHIEF DANIEL BREAD (1800-1873), one of the young Oneida leaders during Removal to Wisconsin, and defenders of Oneida territory purchased in that territory. Painting by Samuel M. Brookes; original photograph by E. C. Nielson.

was to turn total disaster into a major defeat. The first version of the Stambaugh treaty limited the New York natives to 500,000 acres of inferior land. They would hold that only if they could settle 5,000 Six Nations immigrants on it within three years, when the land was to be apportioned at 100 acres per person. The vehement objections of the Oneidas and their supporters forced through some treaty modifications. The boundaries of the area assigned to the Iroquois were shifted so that the quality of land included improved. Land outside the boundaries was set aside for the Munsees, Brothertons and Stockbridges to compensate them for what they were losing on the east side of the Fox River. More important to the Oneidas, the time of apportionment and the amount of land to be allotted to each individual were left to the discretion of the President of the United States. This was an improvement over the first treaty draft, but it only postponed serious problems. The Oneidas were unable to obtain any more concessions, however, and the treaty became official October 27, 1832. Over a century later, the U. S. Indian Claims Commission held it unfair and unconscionable.

Meanwhile, 1,100 people — Stockbridges, Brothertons, Munsees and some Oneidas — moved to their respective new locations. Many Oneidas already lived within the new reservation boundaries, of course, but anyone who remained outside was on the same footing as any other settler. Unless they later moved on to reservation land, Oneidas residing outside the new reservation tended to be absorbed into the non-Oneida population and were lost to their people.

This treaty killed all hopes for the re-establishment of the Six Nations in the west. The last large party of Oneidas to leave New York arrived in Wisconsin in 1836. No groups from the other Six Nations showed any interest in colonizing Wisconsin. Opposition to removal had been confirmed by the Oneida experience.

In 1836, the missionary Richard F. Cadle, by then a six-year veteran at Oneida, was succeeded by Solomon Davis, whose judgment in retrospect seems inferior to that of his predecessors. In his opinion the Oneidas were in desperate need of cash. With four of the Oneida leaders, therefore, Davis went to Washington to raise money by selling the land the Oneidas had just obtained with much effort. The First Christian and the Orchard parties ceded to the United States all land from the treaties of 1831 and 1832 except for 100 acres per individual. The boundary lines of the reserved land were to include all settlements and improvements in the Green Bay area. In return, the United States paid $3,000 to the Orchard party and $30,000 to the First Christian party. Then $3,000 of the latter amount was to be spent on building a church and a parsonage. The rest was to be divided among the individuals who were entitled to reimbursement for expenses incurred in securing previous land claims. This treaty was ratified on May 17, 1838, and reduced Six Nation land to an eight by twelve mile reservation of about 60,000 acres on Duck Creek.

This enormous reduction of Oneida land from hundreds of thousands of acres to a mere 60,000 in sixteen years satisfied the land grabbers for a while. The Wisconsin Oneidas were able to begin to build their society again in relative peace. Methodist missionaries, who had begun to work among the Oneidas in 1829, did continue to compete with Episcopalians for Wisconsin Oneida adherents, perpetuating a degree of religious factionalism.

In 1853, the Rev. Edward A. Goodnough came to the Oneidas as Episcopal missionary. He was to prove to be a staunch friend. When he began his work, the Oneida people were building a more prosperous economic base, but maintained traditional customs to a surprising degree. Most still spoke Oneida rather than English. Their staple food was maize, which they particularly enjoyed made into corn cakes baked in ashes, or as succotash, prepared in an iron kettle and eaten from a wooden ladle. The basic maize diet was supplemented with beans, squash, potatoes and wild game. Mothers of the young people still arranged marriages. Because Rev. Goodnough refused to marry anyone who was unwilling, the arrangements became a bit more flexible after his arrival. Babies were carried everywhere on cradleboards. Lacrosse was the national game. Chiefs announced significant events by sending runners through the reservation. Withcraft was still seen as an occasional problem.

Photographs courtesy Holy Apostles Episcopal Church, Oneida

EPISCOPAL CHURCH BUILDING, started when Oneidas erected their own log chapel in 1825, culminated in the dramatic stone edifice shown in the frontispiece. In 1905, Grafton Hall (top) was added, and confirmation service (1921) was held there while the lightning-damaged church was repaired.

Integration of Oneidas into Wisconsin society proceeded under missionary leadership until the reservation population was affected by the Civil War. Some 135 of its young warriors volunteered for the Union Army, and eighty of them never returned. For a total population of between 1,000 and 1,200, that was a substantial share of the able-bodied young men. In spite of the absence of these young workers, however, the economy of the reservation steadily improved during wartime. By 1864, farms were impressively productive. Men did more of the farming than they had earlier, but women still, by choice, worked in the cornfields which had been their traditional concern. Women were also learning homemaking skills from their non-Oneida neighbors which were appropriate to the smaller log or frame houses which had gradually been replacing the bark longhouses.

The reservation boasted a saw mill, a grist mill, and a blacksmith's shop, all run by Oneidas. The people had several sources of cash income from trade with off-reservation people. They sold firewood and shingles, farm produce, and wild foods such as berries that they gathered. Oneida women wove corn husks into mats which sold for eight to ten cents apiece. They also prepared corn husks for mattresses. The prepared husks sold for four to six cents a pound — hardly a fabulous sum, but still cash.

A perennial problem the Oneidas faced was that every time they began to build a prosperous community, envious non-Indian neighbors started plot-

70

ting to obtain their land and property. The 1860's proved to be no exception. This time the U. S. government agent for the Oneidas, supposedly an individual with their interests at heart, was involved. The agent took advantage of a crop failure and the widespread economic difficulties that followed, to try to bribe or intimidate leaders and other members of the Oneida community into voting for another removal farther west.

The agent encountered strong opposition. Not only was the missionary a courageous and outspoken opponent, but a young chief also waxed eloquent in his denunciation of the agent's schemes. They made a formidable team. Cornelius Hill, born in 1834, had gone to Nashotah as a young boy for his education. At age thirteen, he interrupted his training for a brief return to Duck Creek to be installed as *Onongwatgo* chief of the Bear clan. Now, at twenty, Hill was an educated, intelligent man who understood both Oneida and pioneer Wisconsin societies. He was a church organist and interpreter. He organized the church choir and the Oneida Nation Band. All in all, he was one of the most influential Oneida leaders since the days of Skenandoah. Cornelius Hill was not to be intimidated or bribed, and he could see through the agent's trickery. Through the efforts of Goodnough, Hill, and a number of other Oneidas, the agent's land schemes were defeated. The Wisconsin Oneidas remained in Wisconsin.

In early June of 1866, the old scourge smallpox struck the reservation population. Twenty families

71

were affected before anyone realized that the disease was not measles. Once smallpox was properly diagnosed, mortality and suffering were limited through prompt action using quarantine and vaccination. By the end of June the worst was over, in contrast to earlier epidemics that had often dragged on for a year or more with high mortality.

For the next quarter of a century, the Wisconsin Oneida prospered. Some class distinctions arose as Oneidas imbued with Protestant ethics developed profitable mixed farming on a relatively large scale, and other more conservative families continued to rely more on hunting and gathering wild foods. Oneida constables and judges manned a tribal system of law and order. Individual tradesmen and artisans met most material needs of Oneida reservation residents. A very destructive forest fire in 1871 destroyed, however, major Oneida forest resources. Duck Creek water became undrinkable as the rains washed lye from the ashes into its tributaries.

In 1890, Rev. Goodnough died and was replaced by Rev. Solomon Burleson. Like Solomon Davis, Burleson seemed to be most un-Solomon-like in his decisions about Oneida land. He journeyed to Washington to persuade the Federal government to establish a government boarding school on the reservation and to build a much-needed bridge over Duck Creek. The Dawes Indian Allotment Act had been passed in 1887, and the Commissioner of Indian Affairs offered a deal. If the Oneidas would accept apportionment of their land, the Commissioner

72

CHIEF CORNELIUS HILL (1834-1907), installed as *Onongwatgo*, or chief of the Oneida Bear Clan in 1847, defender of Wisconsin Oneida territory, organizer of the Nation's Band, ordained Episcopal priest in 1903.

would recommend a boarding school to the Secretary of the Interior. The Oneidas did agree. Their land was apportioned.

The government reserved a tract near the settlement center for a school, which opened with a full complement of students in 1893. Land allotment, however, opened the way for a new land grab. Unscrupulous individuals began at once tricking Oneidas into signing deeds or mortgages when they thought they were signing some innocuous paper, or plying them with liquor until they knew not what they were signing. It was the earlier story of unconscionable dealings all over again, but this time with individuals rather than with the nation. By 1904, all but a few Oneida individuals had acquired U. S. citizenship but lost their land, and the 60,000 acres of the Oneida Reservation had trickled away.

Rev. Burleson was not entirely a detrimental influence. Before becoming a missionary, he had studied medicine and dentistry. Recognizing the overwhelming medical needs on the reservation, he managed to establish the Oneida hospital. When Rev. F. W. Merrill succeeded Burleson, he improved the situation by upgrading the quality of the medical personnel. The hospital was originally in charge of the Sisters of the Nativity. Although willing, members of that order were not medically trained. Rev. Merrill placed the hospital in charge of Lavinia Cornelius, an Oneida who had graduated from a nursing school in New Haven. When she was later appointed to the government school, Nancy

74

THE FAMILY BARN AND HORSES of Oneida Tribal Chairman Purcell R. Powless, whose father, Mark, and grandfather appear here with other Oneida holding their fine horses in front of the barn on their Oneida farm.

Cornelius took over. She was a graduate of the Hartford Training School for Nurses.

Rev. Merrill also cooperated to continue the economic growth of the community. Mrs. Charles Bronson introduced lace work, having been sent by Miss Sybil Carter, famous for her quality work, in response to a request for a teacher. The Oneida lace work became more financially successful than beaded moccasins, which were a continuing source of income. With Rev. Merrill's encouragement, a creamery opened which soon was purchasing milk from forty cows and selling butter the year round.

In 1903, the federal government began distribution of almost $2,000,000 the Oneidas has been awarded for loss of lands in Kansas. The award had been made in 1900, but distribution was delayed because Oneidas disagreed on how it should be accomplished. Much of the money seems to have gone for things such as a threshing machine and other modern equipment. A second cheese factory in addition to the church-supervised creamery opened about this time. Inasmuch as there were about 2,200 Oneidas on the reservation, an even distribution of income would have provided a substantial sum to each family. There is no evidence, however, of any such amount of cash pouring into the community. Again, unscrupulous people probably managed to corner most of the distribution, giving little in return.

On the other hand, Oneidas were taking over more and more of the occupations that had been

76

filled by others. The Episcopal Church finally ordained Chief Cornelius Hill a priest in 1903, only four years before his death. Not many years later, his daughter, Josephine H. Webster, took over management of the lace industry. Dr. Josiah Powless, who had earned an M. D. degree in Milwaukee, and his wife took charge of the Oneida hospital. Five of the teachers at the government boarding school were Oneidas, along with a number of other staff members. A Mohawk woman, Rosa Minoka, with an M. D. degree from Women's Medical College in Philadelphia, had married Charles Hill, an Oneida, and came to live and later to provide free medical advice in the community.

As better education became more common on the reservation, and as opportunities opened up for good jobs in the off-reservation communities, Oneidas had to face a new problem that had not troubled them much in the past. Many of the best educated and skilled Oneidas moved off the reservation into the non-Oneida world. For example, the Lincoln School over a seventeen-year period in the late 1800's educated 519 Oneida boys and 487 girls, only eight of whom returned to live on the reservation. Thus, the basketball coach at the University of Wisconsin — Madison, is named Powless and is of Oneida descent. Yet he grew up not at Oneida, but in southern Illinois.

This process was accelerated by the first World War. Over 150 Oneidas enlisted, including Dr. Powless. Some, like him, were killed in battle.

Many of the survivors were reluctant to return to the relatively isolated Oneida community after the war.

Other Oneida were forced to leave the community because of the demands of their new occupations. Chester P. Cornelius, qualified to be a Turtle clan chief, became an attorney who practiced in Oklahoma. Dennison Wheelock, a premier musician, also became an attorney. He moved only to Green Bay, but that was a significant distance when most people traveled by train. After he was admitted to practice before the Supreme Court of the United States in 1919, Wheelock came to spend much time in the national capital city working on Indian claims. Thus, capable educated Oneida were wholly or partially lost to the core community. The intelligent, able individuals who remained found that the pool of skilled, educated people who could help them in their work was much reduced. Many of the people who were left, however willing and intelligent they may have been, were not well educated, which made the reservation situation more difficult.

A new pattern began to develop in the 1920's — one that held both problems and promise for the future.

The Bureau of Indian Affairs closed its Oneida boarding school, barely three decades after opening it, to persuade Oneidas to accept land allotment. Oneida children began to attend public schools in the Seymour, De Pere and Green Bay districts. Half a century later, Oneida students still encounter some discrimination in public schools, such as high school

DR. JOSIAH POWLESS, graduate of Milwaukee Medical College, director of Oneida Hospital. Serving as a doctor in the American Expeditionary Force in France, Dr. Powless died of wounds received rescuing wounded soldiers in no man's land. The U. S. government awarded him a posthumous Silver Star for gallantry in action.

counselors who advise all Indian students against preparing for college. The Bishop of Green Bay's diocese of the Roman Catholic Church purchased the former government school in Oneida settlement to found a religious school. In 1968, after several transformations, that institution initiated its first program for Oneida school-age children.

Social and economic institutions such as the Oneida hospital and Episcopal church creamery were either given up or greatly reduced in scale.

On the other hand, some Oneidas rediscovered their heritage after living away from the Wisconsin community for years. They renewed old ties, made an effort to learn more of their traditions or teach them to their children, and in some cases even moved back into or near the community. An early manifestation of this pattern led to a renewal of ties to New York Iroquois, which culminated in two very different sorts of events.

In one, a delegation of Six Nations chiefs from New York came to Oneida in 1925 to hold a condolence ceremony to raise Oneida chiefs in the traditional manner. Thus, they sought to restore a pattern that had died with the last traditionally raised chief in 1907. The effort turned out to be more symbolic than meaningful in terms of real political power among the Wisconsin Oneida, partly because such absentees as an attorney and a schoolboy were raised as chiefs.

The other event was an attempt to reclaim land in New York State, or to obtain more compensation for

80

Courtesy University of Kentucky Library

DENNISON WHEELOCK, bandmaster at Carlisle Institute, composer, soloist, attorney at law, Green Bay city attorney, admitted to practice before the Supreme Court of Wisconsin in 1911, and the Supreme Court of the United States in 1919.

the land lost. The attempt failed and left behind many bitter feelings. Some people felt cheated by those promoting the attempt — some Oneidas lost property mortgaged to raise funds to finance a court action. Others who had acted in good faith felt betrayed either by those who had misled them or those who withdrew their support. The affair had legal repercussions in Canada and New York, and even caused the removal of the major New York Six Nations chief from his leadership position.

As a result of allotment, only a bit over 1,000 acres was still in Oneida hands by 1930. By that time, the United States was entering its great economic depression. Even Oneida lace makers could not market their fine work as in past years. Mrs. Josephine H. Webster accepted appointment as Oneida postmaster in 1933, to serve for nineteen years. Dr. Rosa Minoka Hill, who long advised Oneidas from her home, under economic pressure passed Wisconsin's medical licensing examination so she could legally practice and charge her patients for the first time. Many Oneidas with less education became migrant harvest hands, picking blueberries from expanding fields, cherries as far away as Michigan, and other fruits.

In December of 1934, after a vigorous debate, Oneidas overwhelmingly voted in favor of organizing, as authorized by the Indian Reorganization Act. That law allowed them to function as a unified tribe and a corporate entity. The vote aroused a great deal of bitterness among the traditional chiefs and their

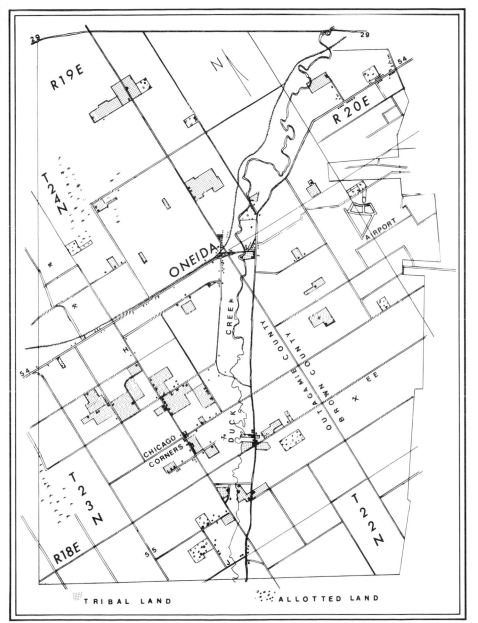

MAP 3. Former Oneida Reservation area showing lands in current Oneida tribal and individual ownership.

supporters, who viewed it as a betrayal of the Oneida way of life. Participation in the voting by Oneidas who were no longer resident in the community was seen as unjustified interference by those conservatives who viewed the emigrants as so uninterested in Oneida welfare that they had abandoned the community to further their own interests. A result of the election, therefore, was to deepen factional feelings among Wisconsin Oneidas, and to turn the traditional chiefs into a sort of underground recognized as the legitimate government by some people, but not by others or by the non-Oneida world.

In spite of factional disputes generated during the debate over organizing, the constitutional government soon secured economic benefits for Oneida people suffering the deprivations of the great depression. The most fundamental change in Wisconsin Oneida tribal fortunes reversed the long historic trend of land loss. For the first time since 1822, Oneidas were able to *add* land to their tribal holdings. Following the policies of Commissioner of Indian Affairs John Collier, the federal government purchased at depression prices some 1,900 acres of land to add to the reservation. This program, too, was bitterly opposed by some Oneidas, and many local residents who wished that the Oneidas had less land, not more.

The increase in tribally-owned land area promptly placed powerful patronage in the hands of the business committee running Oneida tribal affairs between annual councils. The landless Oneidas began

85

to apply to the tribe for house-lot assignments and farming privileges on new tribal lands. Morris Wheelock, the first Tribal Chairman elected in an annual council, called members of the business committee together at his home, or they met at the homes of members. Unpaid and possessing no tribal building in which to meet, they nonetheless wielded real power in making land assignments. With the centuries-old determination of Oneidas, they began to forge a tribal government. Tribal land assignments continue to be a major item on the agenda of business committee meetings today, after tribal governance has been tremendously expanded.

Tribal organization also gave the Wisconsin Oneida people increased control over local allocation of jobs with depression period relief agencies. Tribal government certified Oneida households as eligible for rehabilitation with materials furnished by the government, and work crews paid by the Works Progress Administration.

By the time Wheelock stepped down as chairman in 1939, he could report material improvements to scores of Oneida homes, major gains in land, and turned over a functional tribal government to his successor. Mark Powless, father of the incumbent Tribal Chairman, followed Wheelock for one term.

The Fledgling Oneida tribal government also gained stature quickly in the eyes of the Oneida people because it was able to borrow capital for new housing. The Indian Reorganization Act authorized the Bureau of Indian Affairs to establish a revolving

ROSA MINOKA HILL, M.D., native
Mohawk adopted into the Oneida Tribe
of Wisconsin in 1947 in recognition of
years of selfless service. She graduated
from Philadelphia Women's Medical
College in 1899 (right). She began to
advise Oneidas after Dr. Josiah Powless
died in France, passed the Wisconsin
licensing examination during the depression, and practiced until 1946. In 1949
(bottom) she attended the fiftieth an-
niversary of graduation with three other
surviving classmates, shown with University of Pennsylvania President
Harold Stassen.

Photographs courtesy Norbert Hill, Sr.

credit program to stimulate reservation economic development. The Oneida tribe borrowed money from the federal fund to lend in turn to members, so they might build new homes. When the Bureau did not press the tribe for repayment, however, individual borrowers often failed to repay the tribe so that the program terminated in difficulty.

World War II became a turning point for the Oneida people as it was for the United States as a whole. Raymond Parkhurst, elected Tribal Chairman in 1940, led the tribe until 1943. Then Hyson D. Cornelius assumed the chairmanship and took the Wisconsin Oneidas into the post-war era. Over 200 Oneidas, including several women, served in the armed forces, and many were killed or wounded. Since the return of the veterans of that war and the Korean conflict, Oneidas have been integrated increasingly into the Wisconsin state system, receiving public assistance, etc.

Elected Tribal Chairman in 1947, Julius Danforth proved to be an effective spokesman for the Wisconsin Oneida people before non-Oneidas. Vice-Chairman Oscar Archiquette also devoted much effort to cultivating non-Indian goodwill. The decade of the 1950's saw the tribe file suit before the U. S. Indian Claims Commission for damages inflicted by the Stambaugh Treaty. This decade brought an increasing awareness on the part of non-Oneida neighbors of the situation in the Oneida community. This awareness, coupled with an increased appreciation of native American contribu-

88

Photograph by John I. Griffin

A NOW ABANDONED HOME constructed during the Indian New Deal period with revolving loan fund financing, one of the earlier reservation development projects undertaken by the new business committee of the Oneida Tribe of Indians of Wisconsin.

tions to society and specifically a new interest in Oneida participation and contributions, led to a number of organizations becoming involved in attempts to assist Oneidas in improving their economic position relative to the rest of society.

Andrew Beachtree devoted a year to the unpaid labor of Tribal Chairman in 1951-52. Dennison Hill then served two years before Danforth returned to the office in 1954. During his second regime, an Oneida, Artley Skenandore, won election as sheriff of Brown County. By the time Julius Danforth left office in 1963, he had served longer as Tribal Chairman than any other Oneida.

Most of the years he spent as chairman were frustrating ones for him and for the hard-working members of the business committee. Then the John Kennedy and Lyndon B. Johnson administrations materially increased federal governmental assistance to native Americans and their tribal governments. Danforth's successors have been able, therefore, to obtain programs beneficial to the Oneida people that earlier Oneida tribal governments could not even dream about.

A period of marked and rapid change in the Wisconsin Oneida tribal fortunes began when the people elected a woman Tribal Chairman for the first time. Mrs. Irene Moore won the office in 1963, and served during the year when federal policy toward native Americans began to alter in rather fundamental ways. She initiated the formation of an Oneida

Courtesy Holy Apostles Episcopal Church, Oneida

A CHURCH PICNIC on the grounds of Holy Apostles Episcopal Church in Oneida, with spectators watching a baseball game underway on the diamond behind the church. Single family and multiple-family dwellings in the large HUD-financed Oneida housing project on former church land appear in the background, contrasting with the now abandoned home on page 89.

Housing Authority that would obtain federal funds from the Department of Housing and Urban Development to construct a large modern residential neighborhood at Oneida village. The officials of Holy Apostles Episcopal Church cooperated in turning back to the Oneida tribe a tract of land for the housing development from the area the church had acquired from tribal lands in the previous century.

The tribal housing authority named one street in the new neighborhood "Bennett" in honor of President Johnson's Commissioner of Indian Affairs. Robert L. Bennett, born at Oneida in 1912, became the first person to work his way up through the ranks of the Bureau of Indian Affairs to the Commissionership. He was also only the second native American appointed to the post in a century, although his appointment apparently set a precedent for the future. He is also a prime example of an Oneida who has become very successful far away from Oneida, Wisconsin.

The importance of Oneidas returning to the old reservation area to live after many years earning a living elsewhere became apparent in 1964. That year Norbert Hill, Sr., won election as Tribal Chairman. One of Dr. Rosa Minoka Hill's sons, Norbert, had spent a quarter-century working in Detroit industry. During the 1964-1967 transitional period, he applied the skills of a trained organizer to the rapidly expanding federally-funded programs for the Oneida people. Committees on education, land, health and so on, proliferated as the business committee neces-

Photograph by Henry F. Dobyns

THE ONEIDA TRIBE of Indians of Wisconsin owns this industrial building on its tribal industrial park on the edge of the manufacturing city of Green Bay.

sarily reached out to involve more and more Oneidas in tribal governance.

In 1967, Congress appropriated $745,000 as the Oneida share of damages the Indian Claims Commission held they suffered under the 1832 Stambaugh Treaty. Purcell Powless, a long-time worker in high steel construction, became Tribal Chairman. The following year, Mr. Hill turned his talents to tribal management on a full-time, paid basis. The Tribe formed the Oneida Industrial Development Corporation and set up an industrial park on tribal lands within a larger industrial park being developed by the city of Green Bay.

The business committee also acquired the first Wisconsin Oneida tribal headquarters building. When the Green Bay airport authority extended its main runway, it assumed that it could condemn any land required. A parcel of trust-status Oneida land just off the end of the new runway was not subject to municipal powers of eminent domain. The Oneida tribal leaders negotiated a settlement by land exchange. The airport authority purchased a recently abandoned rural school within the old Oneida reservation area which it traded for the parcel it needed. The authority also paid the moving expenses of the Oneida family that had lived at the end of the runway. Chairman Powless convenes regular monthly and special business committee meetings in the basement auditorium of the former school building, which houses tribal offices upstairs.

The incumbent leadership team has also carried

HON. ROBERT L. BENNETT, former U. S. Commissioner of Indian Affairs, the second native American and first Oneida to hold that post. Director of the American Indian Law Center, University of New Mexico.

Photograph by John I. Griffin

PLAYING IN THE MODERN HOUSING DEVELOPMENT at Oneida, Wisconsin, Bruce Webster rides in front of the tribal Memorial community center building. Bruce and his twin sister are children of Rudolf and Violet Webster.

out two significant tribal building projects. One put up a large industrial building in the Oneida Industrial Park to try to attract an income-producing tenant. The other erected a large Memorial Center in the principal residential neighborhood at Oneida village. This center provides offices for the Tribal Manager and Chairman, small conference rooms, a tribal library and recreational facilities.

THE FUTURE

Signs for the Oneida future are encouraging.

There seems to be no question that the Oneida people will survive into the forseeable future as a distinct social and cultural entity. As a matter of fact, the Wisconsin Oneidas may well become more culturally distinct from the non-Indian population in the near future than they have been for a century and a half since all became Christians. As Wisconsin Oneidas visit Iroquois of the other Six Nations in New York and Canada, they quite probably will choose to reject the leadership of Christian ministers, whose historic advice to the Oneida people has often resulted in Oneidas losing material property and cultural heritage. Secularism and the Iroquois Longhouse religion are likely to gain adherents from the Christian congregations.

Secularization of economic opportunity in U. S. society has already weakened the Christian position among the Oneida. As this trend continues, the steady drain of skilled and educated Oneidas from the community may slow if not entirely cease. The

Oneida Industrial Park should play an important role in future local employment as tenants are found which will preferentially hire Oneidas.

The Indian Claims Commission award constitutes another unifying economic influence. On May 28, 1974, tribal members voted in general assembly to manage it as a permanent capital fund. Increased to $1,171,248 by accumulated interest, the money will be invested to obtain a $90,000 annual income from a minimum $1,000,000 investment. The tribe will distribute $171,248.60 in $176.05 payments to 972 enrolled members 59 years of age or older this year. It will pay 482 members, now 51 to 59 years old, $186.61 in 1975, and continue per capita distributions until 1993, when 154 children, now aged three to seven, should receive $532.65 each. The tribe will still have its million dollars of capital intact to use for leverage in tribal economic development, and to increase after 1993.

The level of formal education in the Oneida community will continue to be high, and not all well-educated Oneidas will have to leave the Green Bay metropolitan area to find employment. General public interest in native American customs is providing a congenial climate for development and should do so for some time to come.

Increasing Oneida skill in obtaining equitable treatment in the economic and political structure of the United States should bring more benefits to the community without the erosion of tradition that was one price Oneidas formerly had to pay for any

100

economic improvement. The remarkably resiliant Oneida culture, which has survived 400 years of incredible stresses, would seem to have better prospects now than at any time in the 20th century.

Problems of great magnitude still exist, or course, and will continue to handicap the Oneida people. There are still U. S. citizens who would like to see total elimination of native Americans and their culture. Yet today's Oneidas are more competent to deal with such threats than were their ancestors. Young Oneidas are becoming involved in their community and increasingly proud of their cultural heritage. They have reason to be proud. Few peoples can boast of similar accomplishments under the conditions the Oneidas have faced and overcome.

"Enduring People of the Stone" is an appropriate name.

Historians and anthropologists have virtually ignored the Oneida people for half a century. Consequently only a very short list of books can be recommended for further reading about the Enduring People.

BLOOMFIELD, J. K., *The Oneidas*. New York: Alden Bros., 1907.

Full of pious platitudes, Bloomfield's turn-of-the-century history is indispensible for the historian, yet clearly biased in favor of Christian missionary labors.

MORGAN, LEWIS HENRY, *League of the Ho-De-No-Sau-Nee or Iroquois*. Various editions, including New York 1901, New Haven, 1954.

A pioneer analysis of Iroquois societies, treating Oneida along with others of the Six Nations, clearly biased by its evolutionary scheme. Also indispensible.

THE AUTHOR

CARA E. RICHARDS received her undergraduate education at Queens College in Flushing, New York, and her Ph.D. degree from Cornell University. She has engaged in extensive ethnological and ethnohistorical research with Iroquois, particularly Onondaga in New York State. She has also had research experience with Navajos in the Southwest, with urban and rural groups in Peru, and in urban New York City.

Dr. Richards is the author of a popular cultural anthropology textbook, *Man in Perspective*, and a number of scientific articles.

Currently, Dr. Richards chairs the Department of Economics, Psychology and Sociology at Transylvania University in Lexington, Kentucky.